DATE DUE

DEMCO 128-8155

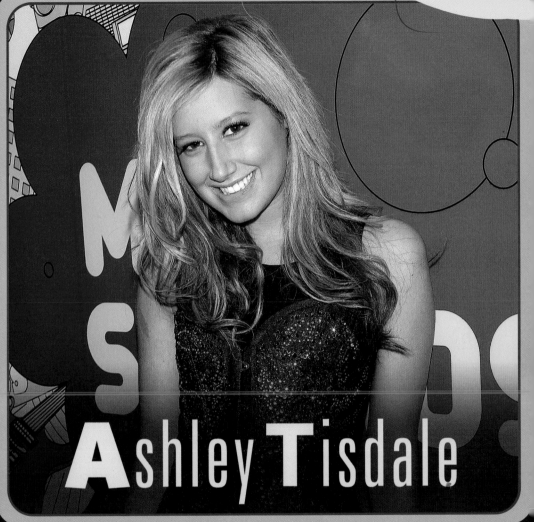

Ashley Tisdale

Katie Franks

PowerKiDS press™

New York

For Dan, who always wins by a nose

Published in 2009 by The Rosen Publishing Group, Inc.
29 East 21st Street, New York, NY 10010

First Edition

Editor: Nicole Pristash
Book Design: Kate Laczynski
Photo Researcher: Nicole Pristash

Photo Credits: Cover, pp. 1, 4, 15, 16 © Getty Images, Inc.; p. 7 © Zuma Press; p. 8 © Amy Graves/Getty Images, Inc.; p 11 © Jeffrey Mayer/Getty Images, Inc.; p. 12 © Eric Neitzel Archive/Getty Images, Inc.; p. 19 © Jason Merritt/Getty Images, Inc.; p. 20 © Ray Mickshaw/Getty Images, Inc.

Library of Congress Cataloging-in-Publication Data

Franks, Katie.
  Ashley Tisdale / Katie Franks.
      p. cm. — (Kid stars!)
  Includes index.
  ISBN 978-1-4042-4468-9 (library binding) ISBN 978-1-4042-4533-4 (pbk)
  ISBN 978-1-4042-4551-8 (6-pack)
  1. Tisdale, Ashley—Juvenile literature. 2. Actors—United States—Biography—Juvenile literature. I. Title.

PN2287.T57F73 2009
791.4302'8092—dc22
[B]
                              2008000995

Manufactured in the United States of America

Contents

Ashley not only acts well, but she is also a talented singer. In 2007, Ashley and her cast mates won an American Music Award for the *High School Musical* album.

Meet Ashley Tisdale

Ashley Tisdale is one of the hottest stars in Hollywood. You first knew her as Maddie Fitzpatrick on the Disney Channel's *The Suite Life of Zack & Cody*. Then in 2006, Ashley played Sharpay Evans in the surprise hit *High School **Musical***. Now, Ashley is more **popular** than ever.

Ashley has been hard at work from a very young age. She has made lots of young fans who look up to her. Let's learn more about her acting life, her personal life, and the fun things she will do later!

A Child Actor

Ashley Michelle Tisdale was born on July 2, 1985, in West Deal, New Jersey. Her mother and father are Lisa and Mike Tisdale. Ashley has an older sister, Jennifer, who is also an actress. Ashley thinks of her sister as her best friend.

When Ashley was only three years old, a talent **agent** discovered her in a mall. Soon, Ashley began to audition, or try out, for TV **commercials**. She began acting in plays, too. By the time Ashley was eight years old, she was already **touring** and acting in Broadway shows, such as *Les Misèrables* and *Annie*!

The thing Ashley loves most about acting is playing different characters. She likes telling stories through them.

7

Ashley's big Disney audition was for *The Suite Life of Zack & Cody*. Dylan (left) and Cole (right) Sprouse played the characters Zack and Cody on the show.

Ashley on TV

After a few years of acting in plays and doing more than 100 TV commercials, Ashley started to do guest spots on TV shows. A guest spot is when an actor appears on a TV show for a short time but does not become part of the show's cast.

From 2000 to 2005, Ashley guest starred on more than 15 TV shows, such as *The Amanda Show* and *Grounded for Life*. All these appearances helped Ashley get noticed even more. Soon, she got the chance to audition for a big part on a Disney TV show.

Ashley's Suite Break

In 2004, when she was 19, Ashley got a role, or part, on *The Suite Life of Zack & Cody*. It was a big break for her to be part of the show's cast. Ashley first auditioned for the part of London Tipton, but she ended up playing Maddie Fitzpatrick. Maddie works in the candy shop of a **hotel**. She also babysits the characters, Zack and Cody, who live there.

The show quickly became popular. Its big success gave Ashley the chance to try out for other Disney shows. Soon, she would find herself cast in Disney's biggest hit yet.

Here Ashley is seen with Brenda Song. Brenda played London Tipton on *The Suite Life of Zack & Cody*.

Ashley and her cast mates from *High School Musical* are very close friends. Ashley has said that her cast mates feel like her brothers and sisters.

High School Musical

In 2006, Ashley played the part of Sharpay Evans in the Disney movie *High School Musical*. Sharpay loves to sing and act in plays at her school. When she hears that people from outside her acting club are trying out for the school's latest musical, she tries to stop them. Sharpay's plans do not work, but everyone learns to get along.

High School Musical became the most popular movie on Disney. More than seven million people watched the movie its first night on TV. *High School Musical* made Ashley and the rest of its stars famous overnight.

Ashley's Music

Ashley's voice is one of the reasons *High School Musical* was such a success. She sings on five of the songs on the movie's **sound track**. The album became one of the biggest-selling albums of 2006. It reached number one two times that year. The first time Ashley entered the Billboard Hot 100 charts, she had two songs on it at the same time. This made music history. The songs were "Bop to the Top" and "What I've Been Looking For."

Ashley loved the success of the *High School Musical* sound track. She decided she wanted to put out an album of her own.

Here Ashley and the *High School Musical* cast are singing on *The Today Show*. They sang the song "We're All in This Together."

Ashley's album *Headstrong* sold 64,000 albums its first week. Here Ashley is seen singing "He Said She Said" on MTV's *Total Request Live*.

Headstrong

In 2007, when she was 22, Ashley put out her first album, *Headstrong*. A person who is headstrong is someone who will push hard to do things her way. *Headstrong* entered the Billboard album sales chart at number five, which means it was very popular.

Ashley is very headstrong in her everyday life. She says she is different from many other stars her age. Ashley works hard to stay away from drugs and drinking because her mom taught her not to give in to **peer pressure**. That makes Ashley pretty headstrong about staying healthy!

High School Sequels

After Ashley finished *High School Musical* and *Headstrong*, she kept busy. Ashley guest starred on some more Disney shows, such as *Kim Possible*. She also appeared on *Hannah Montana*, in which she played her *Suite Life* character, Maddie Fitzpatrick.

In the summer of 2007, Ashley played Sharpay Evans again in *High School Musical 2*, the **sequel** to the first movie. In the sequel, Sharpay tries to cause trouble at the country club where the characters work and hang out. However, Sharpay is beaten again. *High School Musical 2* was a huge hit. It was even more popular than the first movie!

On August 14, 2007, the cast of *High School Musical 2* watched the movie's first showing at Disneyland Resort, in California.

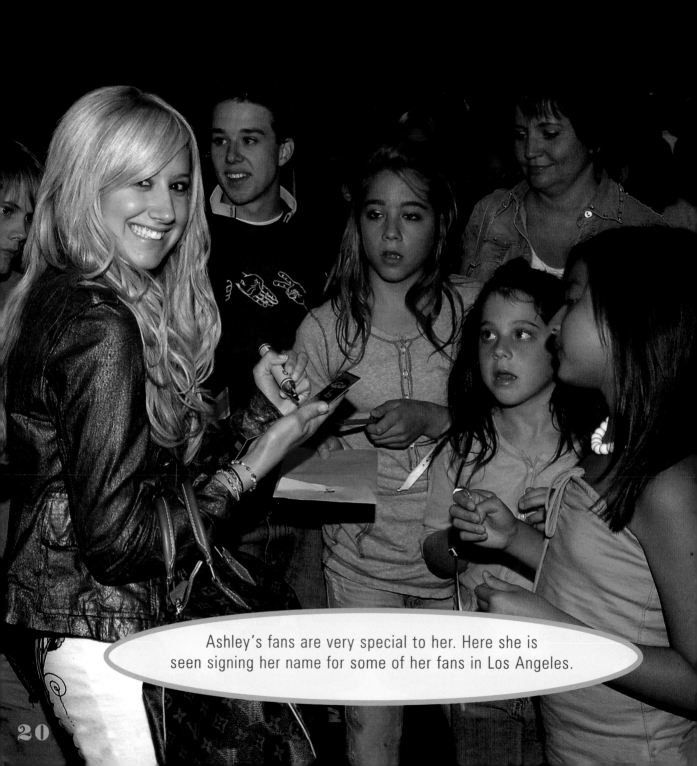

Ashley's fans are very special to her. Here she is seen signing her name for some of her fans in Los Angeles.

What's Next?

The next couple of years will be busy for Ashley Tisdale. One of the things she wants to work on is her music **career**. She loves singing and wants to share her music with her fans by putting out more albums.

Ashley is also working on more movies. Ashley is to appear in the third *High School Musical* movie and *They Came from Upstairs*. With all the **projects** Ashley is working on, she is soon to become an even bigger star. This headstrong actress has a bright career to look forward to!

ASHLEY TISDALE

 Ashley is good friends with her *High School Musical* costar Zac Efron.

 Ashley loves to go shopping.

 Her **favorite** sport to play is basketball.

 Friends is Ashley's favorite TV show.

 One of Ashley's favorite books is *The Great Gatsby*, by F. Scott Fitzgerald.

 Although she is from New Jersey, Ashley now lives in Los Angeles, California.

 Ashley is 5 feet 3 inches (1.6 m) tall.

 Her favorite foods are sushi and pizza.

 Her hair is really dark brown and curly. She started dyeing it to play Maddie Fitzpatrick in *The Suite Life of Zack & Cody*.

 Ashley has a dog named Blondie, which was also her character's nickname on *The Suite Life of Zack & Cody*.

Glossary

agent (AY-jent) A person who helps an actor with her job.

career (kuh-REER) A job.

commercials (kuh-MER-shulz) TV messages trying to sell something.

favorite (FAY-vuh-rut) Most liked.

hotel (hoh-TEL) A place where you pay to stay overnight.

musical (MYOO-zih-kul) A play or movie that has singing and dancing.

peer pressure (PEER PREH-shur) When friends or classmates make
  you feel like you have to do something you do not want to do.

popular (PAH-pyuh-lur) Liked by lots of people.

projects (PRAH-jekts) Special jobs that someone does.

sequel (SEE-kwel) A movie that continues the story of an earlier movie.

sound track (SOWND TRACK) A music album that is made to go with
  a movie or TV show.

touring (TUHR-ing) Traveling with an acting group to put on a play or
  musical in different places.

Index

Web Sites

Due to the changing nature of Internet links, PowerKids Press has developed an online list of Web sites related to the subject of this book. This site is updated regularly. Please use this link to access the list:
www.powerkidslinks.com/kids/ashley/